MBA
17

812.54 Refuge
VINGO

REFUGE

Mary Vingoe

Scirocco Drama Editor: Glenda MacFarlane
Cover design by Terry Gallagher/Doowah Design Inc.
Author photo by Hal Tatlidi
Printed and bound in Canada on 100% post-consumer recycled paper.

We acknowledge the financial support of the Manitoba Arts Council and The Canada Council for the Arts for our publishing program.

All rights reserved. No part of this book may be reproduced, for any reason, by any means, without the permission of the publisher. This play is fully protected under the copyright laws of Canada and all other countries of the Copyright Union and is subject to royalty. Changes to the text are expressly forbidden without written consent of the author. Rights to produce, film, record in whole or in part, in any medium or in any language, by any group amateur or professional, are retained by the author.
Production inquiries should be addressed to:
mhvingoe@gmail.com

Library and Archives Canada Cataloguing in Publication

Vingoe, Mary H. (Mary Helen), author
   Refuge / Mary Vingoe.

A play.
ISBN 978-1-927922-16-3 (paperback)

   I. Title.

PS8593.I55R44 2015   C812'.54   C2015-904861-3

J. Gordon Shillingford Publishing
P.O. Box 86, RPO Corydon Avenue, Winnipeg, MB Canada R3M 3S3

Refuge is dedicated to the memory of Habtom Kibreab.

Acknowledgements

Refuge contains material from the CBC radio documentary *Habtom's Path* by Mary Lynk. I would like to thank Lee Cohen, Julie Chamagne, Mary Lynk, Beccu Fesshaye, and Lubaba Ali Omare for their courage and for their words, without which this play could not have happened.

I would also like to thank Emma Tibaldo of Playwrights Workshop Montreal for her unwavering belief in the play and for her invaluable dramaturgical assistance throughout the process.

Refuge was developed with assistance from The Canada Council for the Arts, Arts Nova Scotia, in collaboration with Canada's National Arts Centre and with a gift from Joan and Jack Craig. Playwrights Atlantic Resource Centre, AD Jenny Munday, provided support and funding for the play, through PARC's Kitchen Table Readings program. Eastern Front Theatre, AD Charlie Rhindress, also provided valuable support for the play.

Characters

INTERVIEWER..CBC radio journalist
PAMELA ROSS.................................... volunteer at clinic
AMLESET ZERISENAI .... refugee from the Horn of Africa
SAUL ACKMAN... lawyer for clinic
ALLAN ROSS..Pamel's husband
MEBRAHTU .... Ayinom's friend

Note

Refuge takes place in two time frames. The verbatim 'interviews' take place after the main event and the fictionalized 'scenes' lead up to it. Ideally the two should be staged in the same space with lighting shifts.

Production History

Refuge was first performed as a part of Nightwood Theatre's New Groundswell Festival in Toronto in March 2013. *Refuge* was premiered by Eastern Front Theatre and HomeFirst Theatre at the Neptune's Scotiabank Studio in Halifax, October 1-6, 2013 with following cast:

AMLESET	Shelley Hamilton
ALAN	Christian Murray
MEMBRATU	Muoi Nene
PAMELA	Natalie Tannous
SAUL	Hugh Thompson
INTERVIEWER	Samantha Wilson

Directed by Emma Tibaldo

Sound Design by Paul Cram

Set Design by Sue LePage

Costume Design by Helena Marriott

Lighting Design by Leigh Ann Vardy

Production Manager: Justin Dakai

Stage Manager: Sylvia Bell

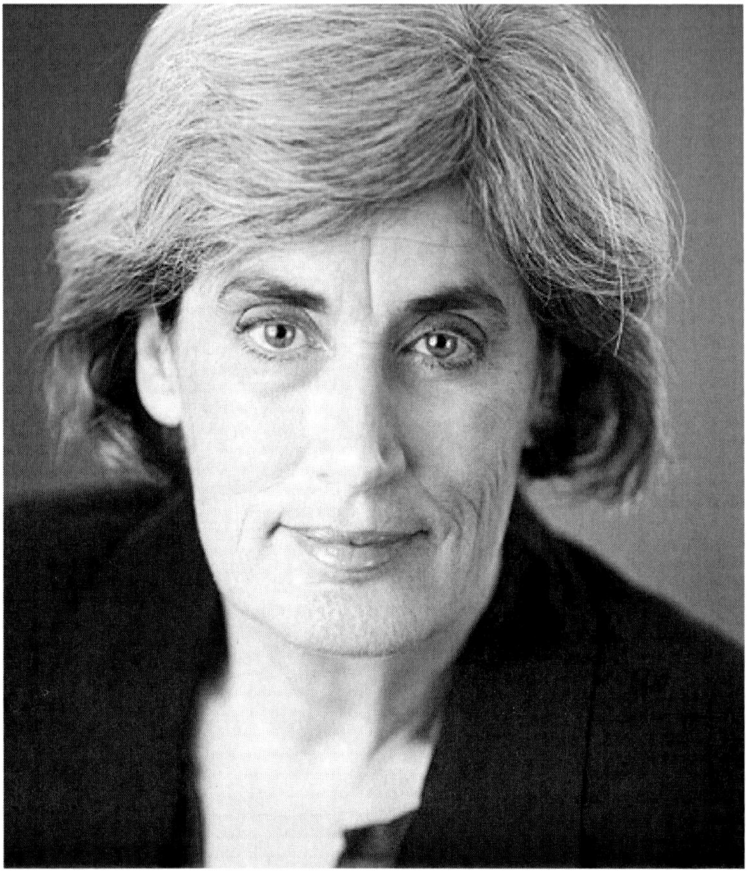

Mary Vingoe

A director, playwright and actor from Halifax, Mary Vingoe is the founding Artistic Director of the Magnetic North Theatre Festival at Canada's National Arts Centre in Ottawa. She is a co-founder and past Artistic Director of Toronto's Nightwood Theatre and founding Artistic Director of The Eastern Front Theatre in Halifax as well as co-founder and past co-Artistic Director of The Ship's Company Theatre in Parrsboro. Vingoe has written extensively for stage and radio, including *Living Curiosities* about Nova Scotian giantess Anna Swan, and *The Company Store* based on the novel by Sheldon Currie. She has directed for theatres across the country, most recently Wendy Lill's *The Glace Bay Miners' Museum* at NAC and Neptune and Catherine Banks's *It Is Solved by Walking* for White Rooster and HomeFirst Theatres.

Mary was the recipient of the 2009 Portia White Award, the Mayor's Award for Achievement in Theatre, the Merritt Award for Lifetime Achievement and the Queen's Diamond Jubilee Medal. In 2011 she was made an Officer of the Order of Canada for her contribution to theatre in Canada.

Act I

Scene One

1st Interview PAMELA.

INTERVIEWER: OK, I'm not part of this. I'm going to try to do it without any of my voice. When I ask you a question I need a complete sentence, if you forget I will remind you, don't worry about it.

PAMELA: Yes I understand...

INTERVIEWER: So when I say, what colour is the sky? You can't say "blue," you say, "The sky is blue."

PAMELA: Yes, the sky is blue, I'll try that as much as possible.

INTERVIEWER: I'll remember and remind you. OK so the first question I want you to, *(To TECHNICIAN.)* I'm turning myself off. I'm turning myself off. *(To PAMELA.)* Tell me, "My name is, and your relationship to him."

PAMELA: My name is Pamela Talwar Ross...

INTERVIEWER: I just want you to self identify right now, for the listeners, "My name is Pamela Talwar Ross I'm an...

PAMELA: My name is Pamela Talwar Ross. I am a member of our immigrant support group here. Ayinom Zerisenai was staying with my family during his refugee determination process.

Scene Two

> *PAMELA has come to AMLESET's house for a tutoring session. AMLESET's apartment is very basic, nearly empty but spotlessly clean. PAMELA has a large file with her. PAMELA watches AMLESET make coffee. It is an elaborate process involving many stages.*

PAMELA: You don't have to go to any trouble really. I'm fine.

AMLESET: You drink coffee yes. Very good, from my country.

PAMELA: Yes yes, I drink coffee, too much.

AMLESET: Indians drink much tea.

PAMELA: Yes yes thank you. I am not really Indian. I mean, I'm Canadian. My Mum's from Cape Breton. That's here in Nova Scotia. My Dad is from India. He immigrated here. Like you.

AMLESET nods.

AMLESET: Coffee brew my country four times. *(She holds up fingers.)* One time *avol*, two time *kale eyti*, three time *bereka*, four time *deridja*. Three time is blessed. One time no good. Three times good.

PAMELA looks bewildered.

PAMELA: Well that's a lot of caffeine. I might have to stop at two. I brought some new exercises.

AMLESET: Yes good good. Canada very good country. Fantastic.

PAMELA: I thought we could try learning phonetically.

AMLESET does not understand.

Use the sound you know, to sound out the words.

AMLESET: Yes yes. Fantastic.

PAMELA: Your teacher in the English class, she doesn't use sounds?

AMLESET: Teacher very good yes. Canadian teacher. Very good.

PAMELA: Yes I am sure she's good.

AMLESET: Many people Russian, Afghani, Indiani like you father. Many people—

PAMELA: Yes many people, many students in your class. Let's have a look.

She takes some worksheets from the file.

This is the 'ACK' group of letters. See, BACK, SACK, RACK. Can we go through these together?

AMLESET gets her glasses. She makes an elaborate display of getting ready to read.

The idea is to draw a line between the picture and the word. See here we have a picture, so what's this?

AMLESET: *(Says the sound of each letter group separately.)* 'P' 'A' 'CH'.

PAMELA: That's good. *(Corrects her sounding out letters.)* 'P' 'A' 'C'K'. PACK. Now can you find the picture?

AMLESET points to a picture.

PAMELA: No that's a sack. 'S' 'A' 'CK'. You know like for carrying. But you are close.

AMLESET points to another picture.

That's 'R' 'A' 'C K', RACK for putting things on, you know. Boy they are similar. What about this one? *(She points to a picture.)*

AMLESET: "PA CA AK".

PAMELA: *(Corrects her.)* 'CK', yes, you got it. That's it for carrying things 'P A C K'.

AMLESET: *(Making it two syllables.)* 'PAC'… 'A K'.

PAMELA: That's better, just run it all together. 'PACK'. Let's do another.

AMLESET: My son Ayinom. He is here.

PAMELA: What?

AMLESET: Ayinom here. Mebrahtu call me, he at airport.

PAMELA: How did he—

AMLESET: He at airport. Police have him. Canadian police. Bad passport. Passport no good.

PAMELA: If he's here Amleset the authorities will help him. Don't worry.

AMLESET: Canadian police very good, not like my country. Canadian police fantastic.

PAMELA: Well…

AMLESET: You meet Ayinom. Very nice boy.

PAMELA: Yes, yes I'm sure I will.

AMLESET: Coffee good yes?

PAMELA: Yes.

AMLESET: *(Points to a word.)* 'L' 'A' 'C H'.

PAMELA: No it's K…at the end, L A C K

AMLESET: What is LA CA…AK?

PAMELA: LACK. That's when something's not there, something's missing.

AMLESET: I not understand this…missing.

PAMELA: It's a hard concept. You see in the picture, the boy empties his pockets, he doesn't have anything in them.

AMLESET: Pockets are missing, yes.

PAMELA: No it's what's in his pockets. They're empty.

AMLESET: Ayinom very good man. I tell him no worry, Canada good country. Fantastic.

PAMELA: *(Smiles.)* Yes.

Scene Three

1st Interview MEBRAHTU.

INTERVIEWER: OK Mebrahtu. *(To TECHNICIAN.)* I was just explaining that it's part of his culture to speak softly. I think it's going to be turned up a little bit over. *(Pause.)* Oh I do. *(Long pause.)* I'm not on mike. I'm just putting my questions in but I'm not really part of it. So if I'm not on who cares. But with Mebrahtu it's more important. *(To MEBRAHTU.)* Mebrahtu do you want to say what you had for breakfast?

MEBRAHTU: Ahm, I had slices of bread with peanut butter and cold milk.

INTERVIEWER: OK, so, so what did you have for supper last night?

MEBRAHTU: For supper last night, ahm… Ah… Probably I had ah, ah a boiled egg, and ah, two slices of whole wheat bread. It's unusual but because this week we are just running here and there. I'm not properly feeding myself.

INTERVIEWER: We're just going to walk through the story. And it's

	all going to be edited. We're trying to tell a story so that Canadians can know. So they'll understand. What I first want you to do is say, "My name is… and I have been Ayinom's friend or best friend or whatever…"
MEBRAHTU:	My name is Mebrahtu. And I'm originally from Eritrea, a small state in East Africa by the Red Sea coast. I know Ayinom from last year. I received a call from the Refugee Clinic to translate for him. He became my friend. He had… But… Because we were living more or less, he was living with a family close to my small coffee shop in Halifax .And ah we're very close, he was a friend, like a son, like a younger brother. We were too close and ah what has happened has really…
INTERVIEWER:	Can I get you to say one more time, just one more time… *(To TECHNICIAN.)* Oh don't worry I can cut it down. *(To MEBRAHTU.)* How do you say his name again? Ayinom?
MEBRAHTU:	Ayinom, Zerisenai.
INTERVIEWER:	Ayinom, I'll make sure we… I get that… Ayinom, was like what?

Scene Four

A reception at an art gallery. The crowd is made up of upscale professionals, a Who's Who of a medium-sized city. There is much chatter, glasses tinkling, smooth jazz in the background.

SAUL: *(Speaking to an offstage person.)* Did you hear the one about the president of Finland who had a parrot who repeated "Brezhnev is a bad man", "Brezhnev is a bad man" over and over? So when Brezhnev was due to pay a visit to Finland he had his guards put the parrot in the freezer. So Brezhnev came and they had their meeting, An hour after he left the President of Finland remembered the parrot. He opened the door of the freezer and took it out. It was still alive. The parrot said, "OK, Brezhnev is a good man", "Brezhnev is a good man." I've been trying… *(Seeing PAMELA.)* Hello.

PAMELA: Hello.

SAUL: Hello!

PAMELA: Hello. It s been a few years.

SAUL: Hello it has.

PAMELA: That's quite a story. I mean about the parrot.

SAUL: I didn't…everyone loves a parrot joke.

PAMELA: I guess he knew the odds.

SAUL: The President?

PAMELA: The parrot.

SAUL: Pamela, well, this is wonderful.

PAMELA: Yes.

SAUL: Why are you…?

PAMELA: My husband, that's his work on the walls.

SAUL: Of course, I'm sorry. Allan Ross. Of course. I have friends who are patrons here.

PAMELA: I see.

SAUL: They get me out of my lair once a decade or so.

PAMELA: He's over there at the buffet.

SAUL: Your husband…

PAMELA: This is unexpected.

SAUL: Yes.

	Pause.
	Abstract expressionism.
PAMELA:	Yes.
SAUL:	Amazing!
PAMELA:	Truly.
ALLAN:	*(Entering.)* Here you are!
PAMELA:	Saul this is my husband Allan Ross, Allan, Saul Ackman.
ALLAN:	The human rights lawyer…I've seen you on TV. Very nice to meet you. Pamela. There are friends of your father's here and our daughter Asha's disappeared. Maybe you could say hello to them.
PAMELA:	Of course. It's nice to see you again Saul.
ALLAN:	Mr. Ackman, if you would excuse us…

Scene Five

2nd MEBRAHTU Interview.

INTERVIEWER: How would you describe him, Ayinom?

MEBRAHTU: Well ah, I find him very strong morally, you know self-made in a sense. You know he was mostly about, mostly, a soldier, I would say. But ah, he was ah, a fact that he was not able to go to school. He missed that very, very much. So he was very much eager to learn. He was an amazing person. He was a very kind person. He was not into drinking into smoking. One time I asked him why doesn't he go downtown or whatever. So when I asked him when he is not having a girlfriend, well you know, life is so hard, he said you know, his attention was on something else. On making a new start. And he really had. He had really, really started. You can see that from day to day. So very good money wise. Looking after himself. And ah and he, he was an amazing person. He had problems in life, but ah, he seemed to be a person, you know he said that was not easily moved. I don't why this thing happened, whatever happened. You know. I can't understand, because Ayinom seemed to be very strong from the outside. You know the way he speaks, his voice, his manners, the way he speaks with anybody. And so I can… He is a very good person, I'll say, he was a very gentle, good, well-person.

Scene Six

ALLAN and PAMELA's house.

ALLAN: So Mark thinks we might have a few sales pending.

PAMELA: Wonderful, which pieces?

ALLAN: "Blue Trombone" has an offer and "Soft Pressure", both the same buyer, guy from the States.

PAMELA: Is it close to what we're asking?

ALLAN: Close.

PAMELA: How much?

ALLAN: I don't want to jinx it.

PAMELA: Fine, say no more. Asha loved the show.

ALLAN: She did?

PAMELA: Well, she loved swanning about drinking peppermint patties at a real art gallery.

ALLAN: I think your Dad was a little taken aback by her outfit.

PAMELA: In India the term 'pre-teen' didn't exist.

ALLAN: So that was 'the guy'?

PAMELA: What guy?

ALLAN: The lawyer, the guy your father had the falling out with over the Sikhs back in the eighties. Was that him?

PAMELA: Yes, that was him.

ALLAN: Your Dad pointed him out.

PAMELA: He did?

ALLAN: You looked like you'd seen a ghost.

PAMELA: I did.

Scene Seven

SAUL's office.

PAMELA: I wasn't sure myself if I would come but seeing you…

SAUL: I am pleased you did.

PAMELA: Twenty years.

SAUL: Twenty years.

PAMELA: You look well.

SAUL: A little grey.

PAMELA: Distinguished. Are you married…now? Children?

SAUL: Divorced. No children. And you?

PAMELA: You met Allan, we have a daughter, she was at the Gallery. Asha. She's eleven.

SAUL: I'm glad.

PAMELA: Yes, you should meet her. She's quite the young activist. It gets her into trouble sometimes at school. She's always got to know where things were made, where the food comes from…what chemicals/are in…

SAUL: Pamela, can I…?

PAMELA: It turns out, I need a lawyer.

SAUL: There's lots in the phone book.

PAMELA: Yes I know. It's just a particular kind of lawyer I need, one who works with immigrants.

SAUL: What does a museum curator need with immigrants?

PAMELA: You've done your research.

SAUL: Years of training…well?

PAMELA: I tutor a woman from East Africa, Amleset, her son has arrived in Canada. He's applied for refugee status.

SAUL: Well, she should talk to the Refugee Clinic. They can help.

PAMELA: But he will need a lawyer.

SAUL: They have a few on call.

PAMELA: I know, I called. They recommended you.

SAUL: I see you got the jump/on me

PAMELA: They said you had the most experience. I didn't doubt it.

SAUL: You haven't changed.

Scene Eight

> *3rd Interview MEBRAHTU.*

INTERVIEWER: OK, OK. Mebrahtu... Um. Tell me what you found in his wallet and just describe—

MEBRAHTU: Well I just found two pictures. One a small ah. Some kind of like a...small ah, like an immigration kind of small shot.

INTERVIEWER: Umm hmm.

MEBRAHTU: And another one with some kind of a background, it must have been done in the studio. He's sitting down in his living room chair and he is with a young, beautiful young woman. He seems to be so relaxed and happy. Ahh...and ah, but he never spoke about anybody to me. He never told me that he had a wife. And he says...in his diary *(Sniff.)* that he was not married, so this could have been maybe his girlfriend, I don't know. It says nothing on the back. It was in his wallet.

INTERVIEWER: Say 'I found it in his wallet.'

MEBRAHTU: In his wallet.

INTERVIEWER: Just say 'I found it in his wallet.'

MEBRAHTU: I found it in his wallet.

Scene Nine

> *SAUL's office.*

SAUL: Hey! Nothing for twenty years and now three times in one week.

PAMELA: You said you'd think about it. Did you, did you think about it?

SAUL: Yes.

PAMELA: Yes?

SAUL: Yes, in between court and budget meetings and planning my Cuban vacation I thought about it. Ayinom Zerisenai. I checked with the clinic. Ayinom has applied to be accepted into the refugee stream.

PAMELA: Yes, that's what Amleset said.

SAUL: It's not clear yet that he is eligible to apply for refugee status.

PAMELA: What do you mean eligible? His mother is here. She's been granted permanent resident status. Why wouldn't he be allowed to apply?

SAUL: He entered the country illegally. Canadian Border Services gets to decide whether he can apply or not. They will interview him first, decide if he can be released. It's a long process.

PAMELA: Canadian Border Services. And they are exactly?

SAUL: Our version of Homeland Security. Been around since 9/11. Where have you been Pamela, under a rock?

PAMELA: I have been married to an artist and working in a museum. Under a rock.

SAUL: I have to ask this. Why all the renewed interest in the real world? Now?

PAMELA: I didn't plan it. It's for Amleset. It's her son. Can you help him? You have a reputation as the best immigration lawyer we have in this city.

SAUL: You flatter me. I may make the most noise but there are lots of others now. Hey, it's a growth industry.

PAMELA: You're cynical.

SAUL: There's a few things I'd like to do if I ever had the time.

PAMELA: What kinds of things?

SAUL: I always liked the sound of the movie business.

PAMELA: You always had cameras following you... What happens when these Border Services people are finished with him?

SAUL: He will be allowed to see a lawyer.

PAMELA: You.

SAUL: If I accept the case. He will be held in Detention until he is deemed not to be a risk. Pamela, it's probably best you get someone else.

Pause.

PAMELA: Young Indo-Canadian arts student meets handsome Jewish lawyer who sweeps her off her feet.

SAUL: Oh no. I am actually thinking of getting out, finding another racket.

PAMELA: They take up all kinds of causes, Nicaragua, Chernobyl . ...You were so photogenic...

SAUL: Hey, unfair.

PAMELA: And so full of big ideas.

SAUL: Please.

PAMELA: Remember how we argued, how it couldn't be about us.

SAUL: Stick to the facts...

PAMELA: That was the mantra/you always.

SAUL: That was the mantra. Stick to the facts.

PAMELA: That's why I am here. This man needs your help.

Scene Ten

4th Interview MEBRAHTU.

INTERVIEWER: What else… What is the last thing he writes in this?

MEBRAHTU: Well, the last thing that he says that—

INTERVIEWER: Say, "Before me I have his diary."

MEBRAHTU: Well, it says he that he got into Canada on, on August…

INTERVIEWER: "I'm looking at his diary right now and I'm reading it and it says…"

MEBRAHTU: Well,/well, it…

INTERVIEWER: Sorry, sorry, there's a problem with the recording. I might have lost that. Can you say that again? Can you say that? "I am looking at the diary of Ayinom Zerisenai…"

Scene Eleven

AMLESET's apartment. It is dark.

PAMELA: Amleset… Amleset are you here?

No answer.

I rang the bell. Someone downstairs let me in. It's time for our lesson. Amleset?

AMLESET emerges.

AMLESET: I not good today my sister, not good today.

PAMELA: What's wrong? Are you sick? Do you need a doctor?

AMLESET: My son very good man, very good.

PAMELA: Ayinom?

AMLESET: No student, no school, my son no school, not know how say good things.

PAMELA: It's OK, OK.

AMLESET: My son go in country, he look for goats, he not know how say good things.

PAMELA: He was a shepherd. Yes I understand.

AMLESET: Army come say, you come with us. He go, he boy.

PAMELA: That was hard on you, on your family.

AMLESET: My son go jail many times my country. He run night, by desert to Sudan to Libya, Libya very bad place, many people die. My son live, he live.

PAMELA: Yes he is here now. He's OK.

AMLESET: He is jail. I see him. He very sad, he say he not come Canada go jail.

PAMELA: In jail? No, no they are just keeping him there for a little while I'm sure, until they figure out what to do.

AMLESET: I come Canada, Kenya. Six year stay camp. My son not come. He army. He come Sudan night. He on truck, many peoples die. My son Libya jail. No Canada jail, jail Libya no good. Bad place. Ayinom get boat. Many boats go down. Ayinom made it. Always he know he come Canada. Canada better place. My son go boat, big sea Italy. Many peoples go down, many boats go down. Many peoples die. Many peoples not make it. Ayinom he make it, he make it, he make it over big sea. He make it.

Scene Twelve

SAUL's office.

PAMELA: Amleset went to see him. He's in the Burnside Prison. With ordinary criminals.

SAUL: I know. There is no special place in this town for refugee claimants.

PAMELA: That's terrible.

SAUL: Terrible is a relative term.

PAMELA: Amleset's afraid, she's afraid that he might say the wrong things.

SAUL: It's a long process. He'll be referred to the clinic. They'll help find him a place to live, get him a job. Pamela...

PAMELA: What?

SAUL: You've taken such an interest.

PAMELA: Amleset is a wonderful person. She's fierce you know when you first meet her. And she won't look at you, but after a few sessions we started to talk about children, family. I guess she started to trust me.

SAUL: It's a good feeling.

PAMELA: My father used to say it was the most important thing.

SAUL: Your father. He was at the opening.

PAMELA: Yes, with his cronies. He wanted to show off his son in law's status as an artist. He's given up on Allan getting a day job. Saul my father and I reconciled, after Asha was born.

SAUL: That's good.

PAMELA: Please don't hold that against me.

SAUL: Not at all.

PAMELA: I was a kid Saul.

SAUL: I didn't/say

PAMELA: Give me credit for growing up without you.

SAUL: I never had any doubt… Pamela, these cases are tricky. You don't always know who you're helping, They can drag on a long time. There's no guarantee of a good outcome. You have to try and not get too emotionally involved.

PAMELA: This from you?

SAUL: This from me.

PAMELA: Will you do it then?

No answer.

Saul, will you do it?

SAUL: Are you sure this time?

PAMELA: I'm sure.

SAUL: OK, OK. Brezhnev is a good man.

Scene Thirteen

1st Interview SAUL.

INTERVIEWER: So um, I'm just scrambling here to make a deadline. It's been quite a day. So. OK. I think the first thing I want to do is…I'm not part of this. I'll remind you if you don't give me a complete sentence. Ayinom, I want you to tell me what he was like. Ayinom was…

SAUL: He was… Ayinom was slight in build, he had a

shy smile, he had a twinkle in his eye, he was very gentle, he was very soft-spoken, he was extremely polite, and he was very appreciative of everything that anyone and everyone was doing for him while he was here trying to seek a safe refuge.

INTERVIEWER: Tell me now Saul, the first time I met him, and my impression was.

SAUL: Well, the first time I met Ayinom I was brought in to start preparing to represent him with his refugee matters, legal matters. And when I first met him I was less occupied with who he was, and more concerned about the outcome because there were challenges in his case, so I was really very professionally focused and almost clinical in my approach with him at that stage, but it didn't take long after working with him to see that he was a gentle soul. And the substance of his case belied his gentility, and I became quite concerned with the fact that I had a very big responsibility on behalf of this man, and I didn't want to fail.

Scene Fourteen

SAUL's office. Three weeks later.

PAMELA: You called.

SAUL: I have news.

PAMELA: Yes. You've had a chance to talk to Ayinom?

SAUL: I have. Border Services let him out. He's not a threat to the public apparently. He's being put up in a hostel right now but he'll need a place to stay.

PAMELA: Amleset has three roommates already. They won't allow a fourth?

SAUL: No.

PAMELA: I know she has applied for a bigger apartment.

SAUL: That could take months. We need something now.

PAMELA: Yes. What kind of shape…?

SAUL: Not bad considering. The amazing thing is that he got here at all. It took years to be posted near a border crossing. He tried to leave the military at least twice. He made a request, in writing, and each time he was thrown in prison and subjected to 'reprogramming.'

PAMELA: How long was his term?

SAUL: There is no term for military service there, there is no retirement. Apparently each time he asked to get out he was more suspect. I guess he knew his time was running out.

PAMELA: Why didn't he go to Kenya and apply from there? Amleset went through Kenya.

SAUL: Maybe he didn't have ten years. That's the average waiting time in the camps in Kenya. He didn't want to put his life on hold for that long.

PAMELA: No, I guess not.

SAUL: Pamela, he needs a place to stay. Right now. Until they decide his case or at least until Amleset gets a bigger apartment. You wanted to help, you can help.

PAMELA: You mean take him in? I don't know if Allan… What kind of person is he?

SAUL: He seems quiet, soft spoken, patient. The first interview with Border Services lasted three hours.

PAMELA: What did they talk about?

SAUL: That's the million dollar question. I wish I knew.

	I'll get a transcript eventually. There are no recordings.
PAMELA:	Maybe we should wait until we know more about him. I'll have to talk to Allan.
SAUL:	He needs help now.
PAMELA:	Like the Sikhs.
SAUL:	Like the Sikhs.
PAMELA:	Amleset is worried about other family members back home.
SAUL:	She has every right to be. They throw ministers of state into prison, journalists, businessmen, family of people they don't like.
PAMELA:	I had no idea.
SAUL:	The outside world has no idea, nor does it care. There is no oil, no gold and so no international media in Eritrea.
PAMELA:	You really have taken this on.
SAUL:	You brought him to me.
PAMELA:	I did.
SAUL:	I still seem to do what you ask.
PAMELA:	I appreciate it. Given the way our family treated you.
SAUL:	The way you treated me.
PAMELA:	Given the way I treated you.
SAUL:	Thank you. When I looked back on it… Air India, your grandparents. It was understandable. And then you marry an artist…I thought you needed security…

PAMELA: I thought I did, then.

SAUL: You have a solid career now..

PAMELA: Allan contributes. He does sell, occasionally.

SAUL: Of course, I didn't/mean

PAMELA: You are a talented lawyer. You could be making a lot more money doing other things.

SAUL: My ex-wife says I have bleeding heart complex.

PAMELA: My father always said you liked the cameras.

SAUL: They come with the territory. And your father never had much time for me.

PAMELA: No.

Pause.

SAUL: Mrs. Ross, this isn't about me or you. Let's stick to the facts…stay focused on Ayinom. Speak with your husband. Let's see if we can get him a job and a place to live.

Scene Fifteen

5th Interview MEBRAHTU.

MEBRAHTU: The only thing that surprised me a little bit, when I said to him why did you tell all the story, he said "I cannot lie." He said, "That would be too much. I haven't done anything wrong." And it's true. You know. That was the kind of situation we had there. The war was very…so many young people, men and women perished in this terrible war. It's the longest war in Africa. It was part of the cold war. You know our country is a state now. You can imagine that was the price that was paid. And this guy, he had no education, and all of a sudden he

	carries a gun. And I find out from our discussion that he was actually a hero. He was a selfless guy. I didn't want to see Ayinom's body but one time he showed me around here, oh a bit here, what I saw was, it's terrible. What I saw was terrible.
INTERVIEWER:	He showed you his chest.
MEBRAHTU:	He showed me his chest. And I could see like something had gone through here, like part of it. He was a very strong person. He was a really strong person. And the fact that he survived and he came here, he had that feeling that you feel that. It's natural. When you survive. There are people around you, who you leave behind, and you come here, you want to be a good person, you want to excel. To get the chance. So that's what makes it more painful to me.

Scene Sixteen

ALLAN and PAMELA's house. PAMELA is lugging boxes.

ALLAN:	Didn't we say the spare room was for your father when he came?
PAMELA:	You know he won't stay here. Look what I found, my grandmother Nana's coral bracelet. I haven't seen that in years. Daddy must have packed it away a million years ago.
ALLAN:	Your father…should have never retired.
PAMELA:	You know he's not comfortable staying with us.
ALAN:	With the no good artist son-in-law.
PAMELA:	Allan he came to the opening, let's/not
ALLAN:	OK we don't need to talk about your father but we did talk about getting a student to make a little

	money…now we are putting up a refugee,…not exactly the same thing.
PAMELA:	We're OK right now… It will be good for Asha. Meet someone from another part of the world. Her school is so white. Expand her horizons.
	She kisses him.
ALLAN:	Her horizons are already pretty wide. She wants to know where my canvas is manufactured. Is it environmentally friendly?
PAMELA:	They're asking questions these kids…it's all good.
ALLAN:	If you say so.

Scene Seventeen

The clinic.

SAUL:	Thank you for coming in Mebrahtu. Tigrigna native speakers here are hard to come by. Mr. Zerisenai is making good progress. They give him a good recommendation at his place of work.
MEBRAHTU:	Yes my new friend does a good job. He is very eager to learn.
SAUL:	It's my job now to help prepare him for the hearing with the Immigration Division of the IRB, The Immigration Refugee Board. I've had a look at the transcripts from the first interview. It says he held the position of captain in the army.
MEBRAHTU:	No no, not captain. He was not a big man in the army.
SAUL:	That's what it says here. Please try and remember it will make a real difference to his case.
MEBRAHTU:	No, no my friend is soldier, very brave, he doesn't like what he sees, he does what he has to.

SAUL: Well this is serious. We will try and have the official translation checked out but as there are no actual recordings of the interview it could be difficult. Can you tell me what kinds of activities he was engaged in the military?

MEBRAHTU: He helps farmers, dig water, make fences.

SAUL: But he must have done more than that. He was posted on the Sudanese border?

It says here he took part in recruitment drives. Is that true?

MEBRAHTU: He says he drove trucks. Young people very poor. They want to join in.

SAUL: And if they didn't?

MEBRAHTU: And if they didn't?

SAUL: Want to come.

MEBRAHTU: They come.

SAUL: And if they didn't?

MEBRAHTU: No choice. They must join in our country. They have no choice.

SAUL: Did Ayinom ever force anyone into the trucks at gunpoint?

MEBRAHTU: I do not know.

SAUL: Was he forced to do anything he now regrets?

MEBRAHTU: He says he fights for his brothers, his country. He does nothing wrong.

SAUL: Thank you Mebrahtu, It will be a long process. We will have to be patient and Ayinom will have to tell his story many times.

The door opens. PAMELA enters.

	And I'd like you to meet someone. Mebrahtu, this is Pamela Ross. Ayinom will be staying with her and her family for a few weeks.
	PAMELA smiles at MEBRAHTU. Shyly they shake hands.
PAMELA:	You are a neighbour. I drive by your shop every morning. We're happy to help Ayinom out while his claim is being processed. Please drop by any time.
MEBRAHTU:	Thank you for taking my brother. God bless you.

Scene Eighteen

The ROSS house, a month later.

PAMELA:	God the traffic! The bridge was backed up to the Rotary. Is Ayinom here for supper?
ALLAN:	I haven't seen him.
PAMELA:	If we're having the chicken, I need to know how much to defrost.
ALLAN:	I didn't see him before he left.
PAMELA:	Did you ask him? It's his night off. Let me just check the fridge. I thought he could eat with us.
ALLAN:	I don't see him, how can I ask him if I don't see him?
PAMELA:	Well you're in a great mood. I have been sitting in traffic for over an hour. Can you at least try and make an effort?
ALLAN:	I do, I have tried. He's always polite but not very communicative. He's got his own thing going I guess. I've got to take Asha to swimming. Back at seven.

PAMELA: He needs to speak more English.

ALLAN: Yeah well he comes and goes. He seems fine. He's on the computer in the den a lot.

PAMELA: I told him he could use it.

ALLAN: Well he does that. Good thing we don't pay for it by the hour.

PAMELA: He has to keep in touch with his family at home. Amleset is coming tonight. To visit.

ALLAN: That's great. We've got to go.

Calling off.

Asha! Come on, we'll be late.

PAMELA: Are you going to be around, tonight?

ALLAN: Of course, I'll say hello.

PAMELA: Maybe stay and talk a little this time.

ALLAN: Sure. I'll be in my studio. Call me if you need me.

PAMELA: Allan!

ALLAN: It's OK. I support you. I am on your side.

Scene Nineteen

2nd Interview SAUL.

INTERVIEWER: Tell me about his life in Nova Scotia?

SAUL: Well I know he was doing extremely well. As soon as he received a work permit he got a job that very week I believe and he went every day after work to the local library where he had help with English. He was really trying to better himself because he'd been given the chance.

Scene Twenty

The clinic.

PAMELA: I went to the front entrance but it was locked. So I came around the side way…

SAUL: I was working late. Cuba next week. Is everything OK with Ayinom?

PAMELA: I'm not sure. Amleset came to visit a few days ago. It felt a little awkward with the two of them, like they should have been in their own place.

SAUL: Well maybe one day.

PAMELA: Last night I heard him come in really late. He was on the computer. I told him he could use it but I didn't expect when everyone was in bed. I wasn't there…it made me a little nervous.

SAUL: Pamela, is there a problem I should know about?

PAMELA: No, yes, I mean I don't know.

SAUL: Do you think he was trying to hide something?

PAMELA: No. It's just…he's like a ghost. He's very polite and stays in his room most of the time. We hardly know he's there. It's a bit unnerving.

SAUL: He can't be/expected

PAMELA: Saul please, he is in our home! We want to help…/ but

SAUL: What is it?

PAMELA: It's just that he won't talk about the past. He's very guarded. He almost never eats with us, has his own food in his room which isn't exactly safe. He has a microwave in there. His light is on late at night. It feels like he's hiding a lot. He doesn't always make eye contact. It makes Allan uncomfortable.

SAUL: It makes Allan uncomfortable?

PAMELA: Well me too I guess, a little.

SAUL: Pamela when people come to this country, like Ayinom came, they are terrified out of their wits, they have survived by lying, by not trusting authority for one second and somehow, against all the odds, they make it.

PAMELA: My father was an immigrant from the Punjab for God's sake Saul, don't lecture me.

SAUL: There was no *Canadian Border Services* in the sixties Pamela. Your father came at a time when immigrants were welcome.

PAMELA: Indians weren't terribly welcome in Nova Scotia. We might as well have been from Mars at my high school.

SAUL: Was he grilled at the Border without a lawyer? No, he came legally and peaceably to this country.

PAMELA: They needed math teachers.

SAUL: Ayinom has been on the run for over three years. He pays big money in Germany for a fake passport. He destroys it on the plane and then he asks to apply for refugee status. They ask him about his origins, why he is running and how he got here, who he paid and how much. He doesn't know what to say. He doesn't know what is expected of him or what the right answer might be. Every country has a right and wrong answer. Sudan does not want to hear what Libya wants to hear. Libya does not want to hear what Germany wants to hear or Italy or Malta. Ayinom decides to tell Canadian Border Services the whole truth. He has been through so much he told me he could not lie any more. He wants to start a new life here.

PAMELA: Well we all want to start a new life…it's just so hard to know—

SAUL: Are you backing out now?

PAMELA: No, I just—

SAUL: Pamela you brought this guy to me. Are you going to abandon him because he makes Allan uncomfortable?

PAMELA: No—of course not.

SAUL: We can look for other accommodations.

PAMELA: No. Stop. Is he OK? Just tell me.

SAUL: I believe he is OK.

PAMELA: OK. That's what I needed to hear. Thank you. Any way I guess that's what the interrogation process is all about.

SAUL: Perhaps.

PAMELA: Perhaps?

SAUL: What do we know about Ayinom's country? Canada has no staff there, no consulate.

PAMELA: Are you saying they don't do research?

SAUL: Oh they do dates, lists, facts. What do we know about being fifteen and dirt poor with no education and going to fight for your country's freedom, like everyone else around you?

PAMELA: Saul you said yourself this country had a reputation for welcoming refugees. They have to ask questions…to protect the rest of us.

SAUL: Of course, of course they do, Pamela, I'm sorry. I may have been in this game too long.

PAMELA: Who is "they" anyway? Who makes these decisions?

SAUL: There is a panel of judges appointed by the Department. They are people from different walks of life, political appointments.

PAMELA: I guess that's normal.

SAUL: They have counsel appointed by the Department of Justice. Counsel who see it as their job to keep people out.

PAMELA: Do you really believe that?

SAUL: A few years ago I didn't but now, this government is playing to 'it's base'. They want to appear tough, keep out the bad guys. But they really have no idea who the real bad guys are. And they know the vast majority of Canadians don't give a fuck as long as they appear tough.

PAMELA: Maybe they're trying to protect the vast majority of Canadians from terrorists like Talwinder Singh Parmar. Maybe they could have used some stricter controls when they let a couple of Sikhs kill three hundred and twenty-nine people travelling Air India.

SAUL: Pamela, I didn't ask to represent Ayinom. You asked me.

PAMELA: Yes.

SAUL: With your background.../we know

PAMELA: Don't blame my background! You think I am supposed to hate refugees and want them out of our country because they're all terrorists.

SAUL: That's not what I/meant

PAMELA: 'We know immigrants can take a hard line on terrorism'.

SAUL: Pamela!

PAMELA: That's what you said then when you were defending a hundred castaway Sikhs who washed up on the south shore like some kind of Disney movie. That's what you said to my father when he hauled me out of your office.

SAUL: He was being an asshole Pamela.

PAMELA: But he knew some things about bringing hatred and grudges to a new land…like the Sikhs who blew up our family.

SAUL: I guess he did.

PAMELA: You were something very dangerous. Something I wasn't supposed to have. There's an attraction in living close to the edge. Aren't you worried about making the same mistake?

SAUL: Mistake?

PAMELA: Just doing it for the rush it gives you? You always loved the rush. Even when you were wrong.

SAUL: Those people on the boats were innocent!

PAMELA: Yes and met by a very powerful brotherhood who wanted to help their people from the old country take revenge on Hindus. Don't you think there was a price for that? Don't you think the newcomers were encouraged if not forced to bring their old animosities with them?

SAUL: Why are you saying this now? I thought you wanted to help?

PAMELA: I do. *(Pause.)* But sometimes I think how do I really know Ayinom is not the same? How do we know he hasn't been or won't be recruited to do some terrible thing here in the east African population? Blow up

	the side he doesn't like or he's been brainwashed not to like…
SAUL:	We don't know…
PAMELA:	You don't believe he committed war crimes?
SAUL:	No I do not.
PAMELA:	What happened to you? After I left that summer?
SAUL:	I played the field, got a sexy Sikh girlfriend…had the time of my life.
PAMELA:	Right.
SAUL:	You weren't the only one who left me. I got hate mail from people who felt I shouldn't be representing these dark skinned foreigners. A man stopped me on the street and said, 'Who did I think I was, The King of the Jews?'
PAMELA:	And what did you say?
SAUL:	I said thank you, thank you because within 24 hours I realized I was home, I knew this was where I wanted to be, right here with the underbelly of humanity. Believe me I had no idea how deep the dark hole was back then. And it made up a little for…
PAMELA:	For…
SAUL:	Your leaving.

Pause.

PAMELA:	And the Sikhs?
SAUL:	Most of them got to stay in Canada… Pamelá what happened to you afterwards?
PAMELA:	I broke with my father. After what he said about you. "The Jews will defend anyone for money."

I lived all over for a while, travelled, then I got a Master's degree in art history. The politics are dead and safely buried in the Italian Renaissance.

SAUL: And are you home now…where you want to be?

PAMELA: My Nana used to say there is only family. Everyone else will forget you eventually.

Scene Twenty-One

6th Interview MEBRAHTU.

INTERVIEWER: Sorry Mebrahtu, I just want to get back to… You say, he once showed you his chest. What did you think you saw on his chest?

MEBRAHTU: Well, like a bullet wound, a bullet wound, yeah. It was a bullet wound. And he was telling me about what happened, small encounters, battles where he participated. How he was able to survive. He never speaks highly of himself, he speaks of unit leaders so highly. The war was so terrible in terms of human life, casualties, and this guy, he survived every encounter. And when he arrived here, it was too much for him, he paid too much, and he didn't expect this. Not that he would be accepted as a hero. But at least, at least that he went through hell. And that's what he said… He didn't do anything. I know there are excesses in the leadership or whatever. This was an ordinary guy. And he didn't expect— It was too much for him.

Scene Twenty-Two

SAUL's office.

ALLAN: Mr. Ackman. Allan Ross.

SAUL: Yes we met briefly, at the reception…

ALLAN:	Right. I've come here to talk about Ayinom Zerisenai.
SAUL:	Yes I assumed so.
ALLAN:	Pamela doesn't know I'm here. I didn't want to upset her. You knew my wife at university I understand?
SAUL:	Yes I did.
ALLAN:	She...she thinks highly of you.
SAUL:	We were friends...at a time when everything seemed possible.
ALLAN:	Well yes, we all remember those days. He seems like a nice enough guy Ayinom, soft spoken, quiet guy. As you know he's living in our house.
SAUL:	Yes. The clinic is grateful.
ALLAN:	I'll be upfront with you. I'm not sure housing a refugee is the best thing for us at the moment. Do you know anything more about him, his family, what he's running away from?
SAUL:	I appreciate your question Mr. Ross but as Mr. Zerisenai's lawyer, I am not at liberty to discuss details.
ALLAN:	Right of course. The guy's had an amazing journey.
SAUL:	He has.
ALLAN:	I mean the Sudan, Libya, those places are hell man.
SAUL:	Yes. How can I help you Mr. Ross?
ALLAN:	The thing is I think I've found something...I haven't told Pamela. I've found something that worries me.

SAUL: Found something?

ALLAN: Yeah, I am not sure what/

SAUL: Did you find this thing among Ayinom's personal belongings?

ALLAN: I'm not a thief Mr. Ackman. I was looking for my old running shoes. We keep them in the spare room we gave to Ayinom. I needed them to work in the shed. He wasn't home. I didn't think he'd mind.

SAUL: And what did you find with the running shoes?

ALLAN: A black notebook—there was a small black notebook, a diary of some kind with entries at the front and names and dates at the back and…

SAUL: …and what?

ALLAN: What looked like payments made to various persons.

SAUL: Do you read Tigrigna Mr. Ross?

ALLAN: Of course not.

SAUL: Is this a problem? That a man keeps a list? It could be anything. It could be money he owes to people, a diary of some kind.

ALLAN: And it could be money he is receiving for something, something he is involved in that we don't know about.

SAUL: Anything is possible. But you have no actual evidence.

ALLAN: The government has issued a most wanted list for illegal immigrants in this country. People who have gotten in under false pretenses. How do we know Ayinom won't go AWOL if his case goes against him?

SAUL: We don't.

ALLAN: So our tenant could become the next name on the list.

SAUL: If that became the case I have no doubt the government will use its considerable resources to track him down. But I cannot discuss this with you Mr. Ross, Ayinom Zerisenai is my client. If you have evidence of a crime you can take it to the police or better still bring it to the attention of the clinic.

ALLAN: You sound like you believe it's my problem. Yes it's a problem for me. My wife lost her grandparents in the Air India bombing because someone like Ayinom was let in the country. Did you know that?

SAUL: I know she lost her grandparents in the Air India crash.

ALLAN: She was a teenager. Her father went on a crusade against the Sikhs. He was obsessed, unbearable. Her Mum left…couldn't take it anymore. Somehow as a student, Pamela got involved with the Sikhs when they landed in Nova Scotia. I don't know the full story. Her father wouldn't speak to her for years. He didn't really forgive her until our daughter was born, then, well you know grandchildren…

SAUL: Have a healing effect…

ALLAN: And you were the guy representing the Sikhs, Back in eighty-seven?

SAUL: I was.

ALLAN: You two were close.

SAUL: Yes.

ALLAN: It took them a long time to reconcile. I don't want her back there again over this.

SAUL: Mr. Ross your wife came to me. She begged me to take on this case. If you have concerns you should speak with her first.

ALLAN: Ayinom was in the army. He is very disciplined, fit. What was his rank?

SAUL: I told you I am not at liberty / to

ALLAN: Not at liberty, the guy's in my house.

SAUL: Speak to your wife.

ALLAN: I would if she wasn't here most of the time. What was his rank?

SAUL: I am not going to answer that.

ALLAN: Look I am just trying to protect my family here. Can you understand that? That I have an interest here. That maybe something's going on that I have an interest in.

SAUL: Yes.

ALLAN: I am her husband.

SAUL: Yes.

ALLAN: You lawyers, you are so interested in protecting your clients. I am talking about my wife here. What was his rank?

SAUL: I can't /

ALLAN: Don't give me that! You have an effect on my wife. You maybe have noticed that.

SAUL: Maybe I have.

ALLAN: So maybe I don't really like the effect.

SAUL: I know / she

ALLAN: What was his rank?

SAUL: That is still unclear. There are discrepancies.

ALLAN: That's not what I am asking.

SAUL: All right I believe Ayinom was a corporal, a non commissioned officer. There is no actual recording of what he said in his first interview.

ALLAN: Thank you. And does he have proof, of what he did in the army?

SAUL: There is no proof of anything in these cases. You can be considered guilty by association. If the organization you belonged to committed terrible acts then you are guilty as well even if there is no proof you ever took part or even witnessed such acts. If they can show he joined voluntarily…

ALLAN: Voluntarily. Don't they know?

SAUL: His initial interview was translated by someone on the phone from Montreal. They keep them in the vaults up there.

ALLAN: Come on, vaults?

SAUL: It's a joke Mr. Ross. It seems like that to us down here. They seem to click their fingers and presto a translator, sometimes their French is better than their English. We never meet them. They're piped in. It's always telephone or teleconferencing.

ALLAN: Aren't they professionals? Like yourself?

SAUL: I guess they have passed a test somewhere a long the way but they aren't necessarily familiar with specialized language, like that say of the military. I have no way of knowing how well they speak their own language, whether it is a dialect or whether they are educated.

ALLAN: What do you believe?

SAUL: I believe what he has told me. After liberation the country became involved in a long series of border wars with neighbouring countries. Ayinom took part in these. He participated in border skirmishes with the Jihadists.

ALLAN: I understand why someone would want to leave but how do we know he's innocent of the things that go on there?

SAUL: We don't for certain.

ALLAN: So you go on instinct.

SAUL: I suppose so.

ALLAN: Do you ever get tired? You have an aura about you. My wife has obviously been caught up by it. Like you are saving the world. Are you saving the world Mr. Ackman?

SAUL: No.

ALLAN: I found a picture in Ayinom's room. It's him and a beautiful young woman. Has he told you anything about her?

SAUL: No.

ALLAN: There could be lots of things he hasn't told you. He stays in his room, he's up all night and he sleeps late. Then he walks two miles to the library for some free language program they have there. Every afternoon at four pm he goes off to the bank. He's got a good job there now. He operates the heavy carpet cleaning equipment. And hauls garbage. Apparently he does the work of three men. Pamela says he sees his mother whenever he can. He's very good at what he does. I talked to the manager. They love him there. Great work ethic. Gets home at one in the morning.

SAUL: Many claimants are like that, very hard workers.

ALLAN: The manager told me he gets off at ten pm. I checked. What does he do between ten and one in the morning?

SAUL: I don't have an answer for you.

ALLAN: No one knows. I am not anti-immigration Mr. Ackman. I realize this country is a fortunate one and we need immigration to make up for a dropping birth rate.

SAUL: Yes we do.

ALLAN: And I realize that most people are just trying to get by but when I read about the kinds of things that have gone on there, in his country, the beatings, the torture, the kind of things the military dictatorship is involved in, it turns my stomach. There's been no free press for ten years. Any opposition is rounded up, they have these jails, on the Red/Sea

SAUL: I know about the jails. There's no evidence that Ayinom was involved in any of these things. He worked with farmers. He fought jihadists in border skirmishes.

ALLAN: Did he take part in round-ups, forcing people into the military?

SAUL: He was not giving the orders.

ALLAN: Depending on the translation.

SAUL: I think there is an area open to interpretation. The country is an armed camp. He tried three times in writing to leave the military.

ALLAN: Have you actually seen any of these letters?

SAUL: No I have not.

ALLAN: My father-in-law despises you Mr. Ackman, for representing criminals.

SAUL: Your father-in-law is a racist and a bully.

ALLAN: But he is my family.

SAUL: Yes.

ALLAN: Well at least we are getting somewhere.

SAUL: What he believed was unreasonable. You cannot in all faith/blame

ALLAN: For such a rational man you take a great deal on faith.

Scene Twenty-Three

3rd Interview SAUL.

INTERVIEWER: Did he talk to you about any experiences, any chilling experiences for him that haunted him?

SAUL: Ayinom did not talk to me in those kinds of terms. He didn't talk much. He didn't boast about accomplishment. He didn't complain about the ugliness that he saw during the years in the military. He would answer questions when asked but he would not volunteer information if he was not asked. And I did often wonder how a person could come through those experiences so gentle, and so soft-spoken, having seen such violence. It did make me wonder about him and about what he went through in his country. He did see a lot of death. Not just death of enemy soldiers, but he did see a lot of his own colleagues die in difficult circumstances, and of course there were civilians who were often victimized and he saw the results of that as well.

Scene Twenty-Four

The ROSS house, AYINOM is upstairs.

ALLAN: I'm outta here, band practice.

PAMELA: I thought you were home tonight. I was going to go to the library, to speak with Ayinom's tutor. He's not learning as fast as he could.

ALLAN: He's not learning as fast as he could. Why doesn't he take language classes with Amleset, aren't they designed for new arrivals?

PAMELA: Sshhh! He doesn't qualify Allan, he's not a refugee, he's not a permanent resident. He's a nobody. He has to rely on volunteers.

ALLAN: It's a big rehearsal, couldn't you put it off? Haven't you done enough?

PAMELA: They still haven't decided whether he is even eligible to apply to be a refugee for God's sake. It's taken months.

ALLAN: Pamela, you say I never bother to look deeply into things but in fact in this case I have. I have been doing some research about his country. The military has committed thousands of human rights abuses over there, there's reports of sexual abuse, torture, underground detention, even something called helicopter torture in the military. I don't even know what that is.

PAMELA: When did you start doing this? When did you start caring?

ALLAN: Since you've been gone evenings and weekends.

PAMELA: I told you, I am helping Amleset with her job applications and I've been volunteering some time at the clinic.

ALLAN: Volunteering, again.

PAMELA: Yes, there are a lot a of new claimants…

ALLAN: Pamela how do we know that this guy Ayinom who we have invited into our home wasn't a part of the problem? I mean how could he be part of the military all these years and not be for God's sake.

PAMELA: Allan they were fighting for liberation, Muslims and Christians together and women too. It was a model for the world and then the whole thing fell apart after independence. Remember Flora MacDonald… foreign minister in Mulroney Government? She said back in 1993 that we had a lot to learn from that country. Now the world has forgotten all about them.

ALLAN: Flora MacDonald! That's ancient history. I can't believe you are quoting Flora MacDonald to me. Where is this coming from?

PAMELA: Saul, Saul mentioned it.

ALLAN: Saul.

PAMELA: Between Saul and Amleset I've learned a lot.

ALLAN: Is Saul Ackman married?

PAMELA: Once, I don't think it lasted.

ALLAN: Just wondered.

PAMELA: What are you saying Allan?

ALLAN: I just wondered.

PAMELA: What are you implying?

ALLAN: I am not implying anything. I am saying you're spending an awful lot of time with him, and we are protecting a possible war criminal who we keep in the house in the room next to our eleven-year-old daughter. How paranoid is that?

PAMELA: Saul is a very committed person. He has witnessed so much and helped so many people. Let's not talk about this anymore.

ALLAN: So do I get to go to band practice? Or do you want to ask Ayinom to keep an eye on Asha?

PAMELA: You are a real jerk, you know that!

ALLAN: Well thank you very much. This is getting in the way of my work and you know it.

PAMELA: Everything gets in the way of your work.

ALLAN: Pamela listen, if a Nazi were staying here would you want him in the house?

PAMELA: You can't compare them, Ayinom was just a corporal, he helped farmers.

ALLAN: And rounded up recruits. It was in his first interview with Border Services. Ackman told me. He rounded up recruits. By his own admission.

PAMELA: You went to see Saul Ackman!

ALLAN: I had to find out what you see in him.

PAMELA: Allan that's crazy.

ALLAN: Ackman admits Ayinom took part in recruiting drives.

PAMELA: Yes those were his orders. The military is compulsory/in his country.

ALLAN: He was just following orders.

PAMELA: Yes he was following orders.

ALLAN: And what if they didn't want to come. What if they ran away?

PAMELA: He would have to go after them.

ALLAN: And what if he found them and they still wouldn't come. Would he have used force?

PAMELA: I don't know.

ALLAN: You don't know, does Saul Ackman know, does anybody in Canada really know what Ayinom Zerisenai did in his homeland? Is there any way of knowing?

PAMELA: Ayinom says he violated no one's human rights.

ALLAN: Now he says that, now when he has a lawyer to tell him what to say. Do you think he's stupid Pamela? Do you think he's going to get all the way over here and tell the truth so he can be sent back to that stinking hell hole of a country?

PAMELA: He says he is innocent.

ALLAN: For God's sake so did Talwinder Singh Parmar!

Scene Twenty-Five

4th Interview SAUL.

INTERVIEWER: OK I think we're recording again. So why was he rejected Saul? I'll get to you say "His refugee status was rejected because…"

SAUL: Ayinom was rejected because /

INTERVIEWER: Hold on… Hold on one second I'm just going to tell security…I don't want to lose this. We're going overtime.

Scene Twenty-Six

The ROSS house. ALLAN is holding a knife.

PAMELA: Allan what are you doing? What's the matter?

ALLAN: It was in his room. And there was this heavy duty extension cord, with a big head on it where you plug stuff in. It's one of our kitchen knives. I didn't know what it was doing there. I was stunned. It scared me. I saw the knife and I am thinking why is this knife here?

PAMELA: You shouldn't be going in his room!

ALLAN: I didn't touch it. This afternoon when he went to work, he didn't say anything. Just now in the basement I found the head of the extension cord… he had cut it off you know, come back and took it out. The cord was gone. The knife was back in the drawer.

PAMELA: Put it down. We don't/know

ALLAN: And all the electrical wires. Frayed. What is he up to? Why does this guy go around chopping up extension cords?

PAMELA: I don't know.

ALLAN: You don't know or you don't want to know.

Scene Twenty-Seven

7th Interview MEBRAHTU.

INTERVIEWER: Did he talk to you about how he left the country, how he escaped?

MEBRAHTU: …If I were to tell you how these people make it. I'll tell you how these people make it. They walk from Eritrea to the border to Ethiopia. You have to do it during the night. There are mines, there are animals, wild animals, there are people who can kill you, we are not supposed to do that, there is an enemy on the other side in trenches. You still make it. If you are killed, you are killed. Somehow you make it and people help you, they take you there. And there are hundreds and thousands of what do you call refugees in the Sudan, and his friends say no, no we have to through Libya. That's a shortcut. When you go through Libya you have to go through the desert, through sand dunes, you are twenty-six, Ayinom speaks about it, in the diary, twenty-six people on one car, on top, with small plastic containers for water, you have no compass, you don't even know where you are going!

INTERVIEWER: Can you…so he would have gone to the border… How did he get there?

MEBRAHTU: What he did was—go straight through the border to the Sudan, taking risk, he could be killed, if he's caught he could be sent into some kind of, we have thousands of islands on the Red Sea, they just put you there, in seventy-five degree centigrade in some kind of dungeons there, and you just go crazy and you just die. And you, you are just buried, you are executed. So he was able to make it to the Sudan. And from the Sudan, it took so long. And he had to go to Libya, he writes, when you are going there, there are people looking after money, there are people who are outlaws, people who have guns. Anything could happen to you. How many people died, God knows. In Sudan. In Libya. In Libya he was caught, you are caught, and that crazy Gaddafi whatever they call him, they put refugees in jail. A lot of them, even now. If I were to tell you… people… The Libyan government was trying to deport refugees from Eritrea and one time it sent a plane full and they, the Eritreans, they hijacked the plane and forced it to Sudan, in Khartoum. They said why would we go home to die?

Scene Twenty-Eight

   AMLESET's apartment.

PAMELA: Amleset, I am looking for Ayinom. Have you seen him?

AMLESET: Ayinom no here my sister.

PAMELA: He didn't come home last night. I thought he might have come here.

AMLESET: Ayinom no here. Not see many days.

PAMELA: Did he talk to you? Is there anything wrong?

AMLESET: Ayinom very good man, very proud. He do nothing wrong.

PAMELA: I know I know Amleset it's/just

AMLESET: He say Canada police no believe him.

PAMELA: No Amleset, it's a long process. There are still avenues…

AMLESET: You like coffee. I make.

PAMELA: No not now Amleset , I think I have to go…tell someone.

AMLESET: Coffee very good my country yes.

PAMELA: Yes it's very good. I am sorry I better go.

AMLESET: My country brew coffee four times, you drink, very good, fantastic.

PAMELA: I am sorry I can't stay.

AMLESET: One time *avol*, two time *kale eyti* , three time *bereka*, four time *deridja*. Three time is blessed.

PAMELA: I don't understand/why

AMLESET: Ayinom come see me. I make coffee. Ayinom no stay. He big hurry. He no want stay. Three time blessed I say, you stay, drink coffee three time.

PAMELA: I don't... Mebrahtu. We'll call Mebrahtu.

AMLESET: Ayinom no stay.

PAMELA: He'll know something.

AMLESET: Ayinom no happy, no *bereka*.

Scene Twenty-Nine

8th Interview MEBRAHTU.

INTERVIEWER: So can you just say, "Ayinom went from Sudan to Libya..."

MEBRAHTU: To Libya through the desert. They just took a truck from Sudan, it took like four days through the desert. The most precious thing was like water, like some kind of water that you just have a little bit of like this. It's desert. Sand dunes. No compass, no nothing. They have some kind of an idea. The driver or whatever. Sometimes it's hot, in the sand, and people just go crazy they die you just leave them there. He was able to make it to Libya. When he arrived in Libya he was caught and thrown in to jail. And if from jail if I'm not mistaken now, he must have told me... I can remember very well. When they were taking him from one place to the other he must have jumped from the car. And somehow you know escaped. In Libya, in Libya. And then that is a long way to Europe, to the Mediterranean. You take a dinghy boat you pay money. Cross the Mediterranean Sea. If you make it you make it. If you don't make it you just go to the bottom. This has been our fate. This has been our fate. Very few people make it. Very few people make it. And Ayinom made it, and Ayinom made it. And Ayinom made it.

Scene Thirty

    SAUL's office.

PAMELA: We haven't seen him since yesterday, he didn't come home last night.

SAUL: His claim has been rejected. They have ruled against him, voluntary enlistment, too many contradictions in his testimony.

PAMELA: Oh my God. That's why… I feel terrible. This is terrible. *(Pause.)* What will he do now?

SAUL: After this ruling it will be very difficult but we still have some options.

PAMELA: I've watched him these last few weeks, there's something different about him.

SAUL: Maybe he knew what was coming. He will probably have to disappear for a while, maybe apply to another country.

PAMELA: Allan is scared. He says we don't know who we are harbouring here. That we don't know all the answers.

SAUL: He's right. We can't ever know for sure.

    Pause.

PAMELA: When my grandparents left on that flight my grandfather wasn't speaking to me, he didn't like my haircut, it was an eighties mullet, remember?

SAUL: I remember.

PAMELA: But mostly he was angry with me for going out with you…a Jewish boy… My father could never forgive you for representing Sikhs, the terrorists.

SAUL: Did you?

PAMELA: Yes. I wish now I had the balls to stand up to him from the beginning.

Pause.

When Ayinom came to the house I thought this is it. This is my chance to be brave. I'll do something right this time. I'm still not sure. Why can't I be sure?

SAUL: There were three men in a boat, a priest, a rabbi and a Muslim cleric/

PAMELA: I don't believe you!

SAUL: The waves are getting higher and higher and the boat is taking on water/

PAMELA: Saul!

SAUL: And the Priest says, 'Pray to the Lord for our salvation', and the Muslim Cleric says, 'Praise be to Allah' and the Rabbi says, 'Anyone take out insurance out on this thing?'

PAMELA: Saul.

SAUL: Yes.

PAMELA: I miss you.

Scene Thirty-One

9th Interview MEBRAHTU.

INTERVIEWER: Can you say that again? You are holding his diary.

MEBRAHTU: It says here that he arrived Thursday August the 7th 2008 at 10 o'clock at the Halifax airport. Well it kind of… It goes back. He says, ah, he entered Sudan on Thursday October the 6th 2005. He has one thousand nafka in his pocket. At the back there is a kind of list of what money he had and who he had to pay. He pays some man in Sudan for Libya. And then 2005 December he says…Libya, he arrived in Libya. And then from Libya he was released from jail. He was in Libya in jail for a long time. And from there he says on the second of June 2007 he reaches Germany. *(Pause.)* And yeah in Germany he works, that's all that he says. He has fifty Euro dollars after passport. And in his notes when I read here, it stops where he arrived in Germany…no when he arrived in Halifax, after that, that's where it stops.

INTERVIEWER: So I have a notebook that stops when he gets to Canada. So you just tell that to people…

MEBRAHTU: Yeah so it says Germany here… He arrives Germany on the second of June 2007… OK that's how he was able to get to Germany and then from there to Halifax, yeah 2008 August the seventh Thursday. It stops right there.

INTERVIEWER: And Mebrahtu, I'll also get you to say, so I can put it on top, "I'm reading from a diary of his…"

MEBRAHTU: Yes.

INTERVIEWER: Just say that/

MEBRAHTU: I'm reading from a diary of Ayinom Zerisenai…

INTERVIEWER: And it says…

MEBRAHTU: And it says that it stops when, he arrived in Canada.

Scene Thirty-Two

The ROSS house.

PAMELA: *(Distraught.)* Allan, did you call someone? The government number on the internet where you can say if you think someone is suspicious. Did you call them?

ALLAN: No, no, I thought about it but no I didn't call anyone.

PAMELA: Do you swear to me you didn't call?

ALLAN: I swear.

PAMELA: My God Allan! Where did he go? Why didn't he come home last night?

ALLAN: I asked him about the cord.

PAMELA: What?

ALLAN: I asked him about the cord.

PAMELA: I told you!

ALLAN: I didn't trust him. I started to imagine car bombs and IEDS. We've seen so much on the news lately. He was on his way from the bathroom and I just asked him, I said, what are you doing with that cord? He just looked at me. I'm not sure he understood. Why did you cut it off like that? I don't know if he understood. He was just outside the bathroom door, like he was pinned to it. I got angry. I said he couldn't go around cutting up extension cords. He just looked at me. He said he was sorry. He said very sorry for the problem. Problem. That was the word he used.

Scene Thirty-Three

10th Interview MEBRAHTU.

INTERVIEWER: Did you talk to him after he had heard that he was going to be deported?

MEBRAHTU: Well after the rejection, after, after we got the rejection we had to go to the Refugee clinic and they had to read to him you know how the whole thing works…they said and this could happen, this could happen, this could happen...that he could go and hide in the church, it could be four years, and he said, "Oh what kind of life is that?" They said he could go to Toronto or Calgary and disappear. And he said but it would be like the life of a mouse, and he said, that's another life, what kind of life is this? And they said we are going, you know to appeal, you know, a judicial review, and it's going to be this, and it's going to be this. And they said when you go to the Canadian Services, Border Services, a person is going to ask you, you know, and he is going to see whether or not, they can depend on you, that you show up when they ask you to go to the airport, right? And that's when he said, 'so that's the last thing?'

INTERVIEWER: The last thing?

MEBRAHTU: It was clue. That was enough. He knew, he didn't trust anybody, not Mr. Ackman, not me, not even his mother. He said right on the moment. I was saying to him ah it's not a big thing, I have seen so many things worse than this. But Ayinom at that moment he must have decided because, he asked if he could stay at the store that night. He said he needed to be alone. My Somali guy was away so I said he could stay there. I had to go home early because the next day we were going to go with him, I was going to go with him to Border Services to translate the next day. We had snow that night, a lot of snow, it took me like, at ten o'clock in the morning I was able to arrive at the store, because I had to shovel all the snow by my own place where I live, and by the store I had to park my car somewhere and I go there and I found all this snow in front of the door piled up like this, and I couldn't see any footprints. And I said this is something unusual, what is this? Where did everybody go? Where are all the people? I had one guy from Haiti, I have one guy from Somalia, and that night I had Ayinom. I couldn't see footprints. I just felt the first time, I felt a little bit uneasy. Somehow, you know, my, my, I went on top of the ah, the snow, it was really a lot of snow, I opened the door, just by where I have the store I found this piece of paper. A small piece of paper, I took it out, and it says, upstairs there is a note for you before you can do anything, go upstairs and have a look at the paper, he said, your respecting, loving brother, Ayinom.

So I went upstairs, and I found his note… And I started screaming, it was so loud that Estevan from Haiti had to come, and he said, "Is it fire, what happened?" And I said, something happened, something bad happened, something bad happened, so loud, and screaming I don't know what to do. They told me to, you know call the police. I called the police and they came, and I told them. The police said people do that and he might be hiding somewhere or whatever he understands right. But I said I know that Ayinom has done it, when I person says to you goodbye, when a person leaves you his bank card there, his wallet, his belts, he had three belts, his best pants over there, you see, when you see money there… You have to, you have to. I knew that it happened, I had no question at all, that evening at nine o'clock he went out…and that was the last time.

INTERVIEWER: And in the woods behind the library, can you say that?

MEBRAHTU: It was just behind Clayton Park Junior High. There was a small—but there was a small footpath. So that's how we, because he was going there everyday right? To Keshen library. He must have seen all the trees, they were all thin right? In order to do this thing you need a big tree right? And he found one. And I know, I found out later on, what he used even, what kind of rope he used, it was an electrical cord I know that, a big heavy cord with the end cut off. I don't know, but I am quite sure it was that night, I am quite sure it was that night. The way he wrote the last note, it's so clear, it is so clear.

INTERVIEWER: Why do you think he said that to you?

MEBRAHTU: He respected me very much. But in the end, he didn't trust me, I felt…

INTERVIEWER: Um…

MEBRAHTU: I really feel bad.

INTERVIEWER: I know you do. Ah… You can't blame yourself though. Um.

MEBRAHTU: The next day they told us he has been found, they even found, they even brought a key from his pocket, a key for the place I lent him for the night, he locked…when he left he locked the place and he went.

Scene Thirty-Four

5th Interview SAUL.

INTERVIEWER: If you could talk to him now. I'm actually going to ask you to…to talk to him.

SAUL: What is the question?

INTERVIEWER: What would you say to Ayinom if you could talk to him?

SAUL: If I could speak to him now, I would tell him that in the most peculiar sort of way, I understand his actions. I've always regarded suicide, in some contexts, I have always regarded suicide, the taking of one's own life, the opting out of life, as a genuine option to life. I don't always regard suicide as the act of insanity or severe depression, although I suppose it can be that. I have always identified another context for suicide and that is as a genuine choice.

Scene Thirty-Five

AMLESET's kitchen.

PAMELA: I am so sorry.

AMLESET: Ayinom do terrible thing. People not kill themselves in my country.

PAMELA: He must have felt he had no choice.

AMLESET: It is like a torture. But the next day a student he find. I know that he has done it, on this you know, that was my feeling, right?

PAMELA: Yes.

AMLESET: There is LACH.

PAMELA: I don't understand.

AMLESET: Something not here, missing…pockets LACH.

PAMELA: I don't…oh…missing pockets…the boy…in the picture…yes.

AMLESET: I wait many years Ayinom to come.

Pause.

He come. He angry. He not say goodbye.

PAMELA: Amleset…Amleset…

AMLESET: I wait so long…

PAMELA: Yes.

AMLESET: I tell him I make big letter for apartment. Good for us. Canada. He say no more wait.

Pause.

Ayinom no say goodbye. I wait so long. The boy in picture. He has no mother. Now I have no son.

Scene Thirty-Six

6th Interview SAUL.

SAUL: If I could talk to Ayinom now, I would say that I disagree with his decision, but I admire his bravery, and I admire his commitment to his personal principle that he would never allow himself to be returned to his home country where he would face certain torture and death when it came, would be a relief.

INTERVIEWER: Would you tell him that you missed him?

SAUL: I'm not there yet. I am not there yet. I'm sorry. Please excuse me. There are others waiting.

The stage darkens.

The End.